EXPLORING THE SCIENCE OF NATURE

The Nature and Science of
SUMMER

Jane Burton and Kim Taylor

Gareth Stevens Publishing
MILWAUKEE

For a free color catalog describing Gareth Stevens Publishing's list of high-quality books and multimedia programs, call 1-800-542-2595 (USA) or 1-800-461-9120 (Canada). Gareth Stevens Publishing's Fax: (414) 225-0377.

Library of Congress Cataloging-in-Publication Data

Burton, Jane.
The nature and science of summer / by Jane Burton and Kim Taylor.
p. cm. — (Exploring the science of nature)
Includes bibliographical references and index.
ISBN 0-8368-2189-0 (lib. bdg.)
1. Summer—Juvenile literature. I. Taylor, Kim.
II. Title. III. Series: Burton, Jane.
Exploring the science of nature.
QB637.6.B874   1999
508.2—dc21   99-30126

First published in North America in 1999 by
Gareth Stevens Publishing
1555 North RiverCenter Drive, Suite 201
Milwaukee, Wisconsin 53212 USA

This U.S. edition © 1999 by Gareth Stevens, Inc. Created with original © 1999 by White Cottage Children's Books. Text © 1999 by Kim Taylor. Photographs © 1999 by Jane Burton, Kim Taylor, and Mark Taylor. The photographs on pages 10 (*above*) and 19 (*below, left*) are by Jan Taylor. The photograph on page 23 (*top, left*) is by Gary Huggins. Conceived, designed, and produced by White Cottage Children's Books, 29 Lancaster Park, Richmond, Surrey TW10 6AB, England. Additional end matter © 1999 by Gareth Stevens, Inc.

The rights of Jane Burton and Kim Taylor to be identified as the authors of this work have been asserted by them in accordance with the Copyright, Design and Patents Act 1988. Educational consultant, Jane Weaver; scientific adviser, Dr. Jan Taylor.

Printed in the United States of America

1 2 3 4 5 6 7 8 9 03 02 01 00 99

Contents

Words that appear in the glossary are printed in **boldface** type the first time they occur in the text.

The Meaning of Summer

Summer is a time of plenty. Fresh green grass and leaves appear for many animals to eat. Insects, which can be pesky to humans, are everywhere. They provide a feast for certain animals.

Summer is the warmest of the four seasons because the Sun is more directly overhead than at other times of the year. The Sun's rays do not have to pass through as much of Earth's atmosphere as they do in the other seasons. Therefore, the rays lose less heat before reaching the ground.

Earth's axis is tilted at 23 degrees. As Earth orbits the Sun, it gradually moves to a position where the tilt of its axis is toward the Sun. The date on which the northern end of Earth's axis leans directly toward the Sun is June 20 (or 21), the summer **solstice**. This date marks the official start of summer in the Northern **Hemisphere**.

When the northern end of Earth's axis tilts toward the Sun, the southern end of the axis tilts away from the Sun. So, when summer begins in the Northern Hemisphere, winter begins in the Southern Hemisphere.

The four seasons of spring, summer, autumn, and winter occur only in **temperate** regions of the world. The **tropics** experience only wet and dry seasons. Just two seasons occur in the **polar** regions — a brief summer and a long winter.

Above: Summer in the high mountains is short. Flowers set seed quickly.

Top: The tiger lily is a hardy summer flower.

Opposite: A mother horse and her foal enjoy a summer day beneath a flowering chestnut tree.

Below: The snow will soon return to the mountains to cover these western anemone seed heads.

Dewy Mornings

Top: A dewdrop can form on each tiny hair of a clover leaf.

Midsummer nights can be cool — especially when the sky is clear. If there are no clouds to insulate the Earth, the ground cools quickly, forming **dew**. Dew is moisture in the form of tiny water droplets. Grass and other vegetation can become covered in heavy dew. The water does not come from the sky; it comes from the ground.

Dew forms when the air contains water **vapor**. Imagine a hot summer day when the Sun blazes onto the ground. The soil becomes dry because the Sun's heat causes the moisture in it to **evaporate**. That moisture, in the form of vapor, is now a part of the warm daytime air.

As the Sun sets, the ground starts to cool. The air next to it also cools. Cool air cannot hold as much water vapor as warm air, and a point exists

Right: Dewdrops condense on the petals of creeping phlox.

Left: The pointed tip of each blade of grass glistens with its own drop of water.

at which the air becomes **saturated**. It cannot hold any more vapor. This is called the **dew point**, the point at which dew starts to form. Any further cooling of the air causes even more dew to form.

Dew forms close to the ground because that is where the air is coolest and also where the most water vapor exists. The water vapor **condenses** into round drops, particularly on the edges and points of leaves. The drops grow gradually and can reach 0.08-0.12 inch (2-3 millimeters) across. Because dew forms without splashing or other disturbances, dewy grass can hold more water than rain-soaked grass.

Left: Sleeping dragonflies, such as this one, collect dew on their wings during the night. Dragonflies must wait until the morning Sun dries the dew before they can fly.

Shimmering Water

Top: The sandhopper, a tiny crustacean, has strong hind legs for hopping. It can swim as well as hop.

In summer, the Sun warms the surface of the ocean. Close to the shore, the water is warmed further as the tide comes in over sun-baked rocks and sand. Shimmering tide pools on a summer day come alive with sea creatures. Crabs, prawns, shrimps, and many other types of sea life need warm water in which to **breed**. Female crabs and prawns lay large numbers of tiny eggs, which they carry around with them until the eggs hatch. Other animals, such as whelks, attach their eggs to rocks or seaweed and leave them there.

On the shore itself are piles of rotting seaweed, deposited there by winter storms. The seaweed forms a breeding ground for numerous shore flies.

Right: The incoming tide on a summer day washes warm water over a cluster of sea anemones. The anemones extend pink tentacles as the water covers them.

The smelly seaweed becomes thick with fly maggots, and, if there is an exceptionally high tide, rafts of seaweed may wash out to sea. The floating seaweed attracts various kinds of fish, such as gray mullet, that swim around slowly, sucking the juicy maggots from the surface.

High tides may also disturb sandhoppers, which normally stay beneath stones or buried in the sand. As the seawater advances up the beach, the sandhoppers are driven out from their hiding places. They march ahead of the oncoming waters, like a retreating army. Scientists do not know why sandhoppers scramble to keep ahead of the tide because the tiny crustaceans are at home in the water and swim very well.

Left: A female shore crab carries a mass of eggs under her tail. The eggs will hatch in the warm water of a tide pool.

Above: Seaweed fly maggots live among rotting seaweed. The heat of the summer Sun makes the maggots grow quickly.

Below: An army of sandhoppers marches up a rock ahead of the advancing tide.

Summer Drought

Top: The seeds of the Australian banksia are contained in hard cases, embedded in fireproof cones.

Above: This mud pool in Australia dried out quickly, stranding hundreds of tadpole shrimps. Luckily, the shrimps already laid their eggs. The eggs will survive for years in the sun-baked mud.

Right: There is very little for these zebras to eat during the dry season in Africa. They wait, thin and hungry, for the rains to come and the grass to grow again.

Summer droughts are particularly hard on animals with moist skin, such as slugs, snails, and frogs. These animals are active only at night, when there may be just enough moisture in the air to keep their bodies from drying out. In severe drought, some animals **estivate**. They find a place to hide until the rains return.

A summer drought is like the dry season in warm climates. In many parts of the world, the seasons depend much more on rainfall than on anything else. During the dry season in these climates, leaves fall off the trees, and many plants die. Puddles and ponds dry out, and mud bakes in the Sun until it is hard. Instead of being green and lush, the entire land is brown.

Left: Summer droughts make gorse bushes extremely dry. Fire can completely destroy a gorse bush, but its seeds lying on the ground will start to grow when the rains return.

Below: The bark of the ponderosa pine has several fireproof layers. The outside layers may get burned, but the inner layers remain undamaged, protecting the wood underneath.

The threat of fire is great during the dry season in warm climates. Fire can sweep over the land, killing everything in its path. Fires are often started due to careless acts by people, but dry-season fires can also be started by lightning.

In areas where fires are a regular occurrence, plants and animals have adapted so they can survive. Bigger animals and birds escape by running and flying away. Smaller animals burrow into the ground. Trees, of course, cannot move out of the way, so some of them grow thick, fire-resistant bark. Some trees also produce seeds in fireproof pods, nuts, or cones.

A Canopy of Leaves

Top: Camellia bushes grow in shady places. Their leaves are dark green, like those of many other shade-loving plants.

Above: Veins in leaves carry water to the cells and take away nutrients that the leaves make.

Right: In summer, sunlight reaches the ground beneath trees only in small patches. Most of the sunlight is used by the leaves for photosynthesis.

The color of early summer in temperate climates is green. The grass is green, the bushes are green, and the trees are green. The greens of spring come in many shades, and the countryside is a patchwork of these colors. By summer, the green becomes much more uniform. The color of the pigment **chlorophyll** becomes prominent.

Chlorophyll in leaves collects light from the Sun. During a process that occurs in plants called **photosynthesis**, the Sun's energy transforms **carbon dioxide** and water into sugar. Sugar is a simple **carbohydrate**, and plants use it to make the more complicated carbohydrates from which their roots, stems, branches, and leaves form.

Above: In order to grow, grass collects light from the Sun. Therefore, when a rabbit eats the grass, it also gets energy from the Sun.

Above: Some plants, like this redwood sorrel, grow only in shady places. Because there is so little light beneath trees, the sorrel does not grow very large.

It is an amazing fact that the very solid and enormous structure of a tree forms mainly from carbon dioxide gas in the air.

Sunshine contains light of all the colors of the rainbow, mixed together. Plants use all these colors, except green, for photosynthesis. Green light does not help the chemical process. The other colors are absorbed by leaves, but the unusable green is reflected. The green of summer is actually the shade of green that is *least* useful to plants.

Plants in temperate regions undergo most of their photosynthesis in summer because more light is available at that time than in any other season. Not only is the Sun's light strongest in summer, but day length is also the longest.

Scents and Colors

Top: The bright yellow flowers of California glory stand out against dark green leaves.

Summer flowers come in almost every color, ranging from pure white to the deepest purple — but there are very few green flowers. This is because most flowers need to stand out against their green, leafy background in order to be seen by insects and other animals.

The colors of flowers attract insects that carry **pollen** from flower to flower. Pollen from one flower **fertilizes** another flower of the same **species** to produce seeds. The seeds, of course, grow into new plants.

Insects are not the only animals that pollinate flowers. Many flowers are specially constructed to be pollinated by birds, and some flowers are pollinated by bats. Bird-pollinated flowers are brightly colored because birds rely on their sight

Right: Collecting pollen from flowers during summer can be dangerous for insects. Camouflaged spiders, such as this crab spider, lurk in some flowers to pounce on visiting bees.

14

to find the flowers. Birds can see bright red clearly, so many bird-pollinated flowers are red. Insects cannot see red very well, and so few insect-pollinated flowers are red. Instead, they may be yellow or blue.

Flowers do not rely just on color to attract pollinators. Scent is also important. Some flowers open at night and pour a pleasant fragrance into the night air. Moths or bats follow the scent through the darkness to the flowers.

Not all flowers have a pleasant scent, however. Flowers pollinated by flies may smell like rotten meat to attract their own special pollinators.

Above: White bryony relies on one kind of solitary bee to pollinate its flowers. The bryony does not need bright flowers to attract any other types of insects.

Left: Foxglove and ox-eye daisies advertise themselves with bright colors. They need to be easily seen by insects.

The Sounds of Summer

Top: The wings of this male speckled bush-cricket are not built for flying. They are designed to produce a loud click when rubbed together. People do not hear the click because the sound is **ultrasonic**.

The air on a fine summer day is full of the sounds of insects. Stand still and listen on a windless day in a **deciduous** forest — far from traffic noise — and you will hear a steady hum. The hum is caused by the beating of countless insect wings. Bees and wasps go about their important business, flying straight and purposefully. Male hoverflies perch or hover, waiting for females to fly past.

Male hoverflies can hang in the air, their bodies motionless, so that their eyes can best detect any movement. As soon as a flying insect comes in the range of a hoverfly's vision — which may be within approximately 3-6 feet (1-2 meters) — the hoverfly chases it. If the male hoverfly determines that the insect is not a female hoverfly, he returns to his hovering position.

Right: Mosquitoes breed in water. This female is emerging from her **pupa** onto the surface of a pond. Another female flies away. Mosquitoes beat their wings rapidly, which makes a high-pitched whine.

16

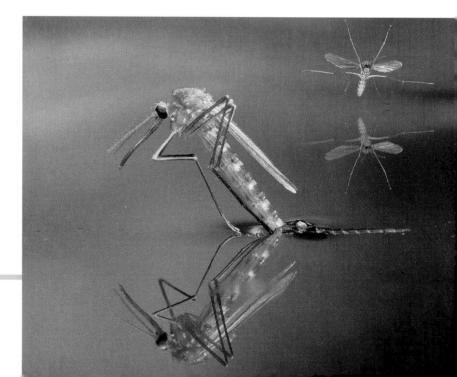

Left: The male hoverfly beats its wings rapidly as it hovers. This motion creates a steady hum.

Hoverflies do not hover for very long at one time. Hovering is very hard work, and the flies need to rest. While resting on twigs or leaves, they keep their body temperature up by vibrating their wing muscles.

This muscle vibration is not visible to the human eye, but people hear it as a steady whine. The sound comes from the muscle movement of perched hoverflies. The continuous whine, from thousands of male hoverflies, makes a strong contribution to the sounds of the natural world in summer.

Above: In summer, when a male hoverfly finds a female, he mates with her. She can then lay eggs.

Left: This hoverfly is refueling between flights. Hoverflies add to the sounds of summer when they perch or hover.

17

The background noise of these humming wings can be heard only by people when few competing sounds are present. Male crickets make chirping noises by rubbing ridged patches located on their wings together. These sounds can drown out the humming sound of a hoverfly.

Crickets make their chirping noises mostly at night. Male grasshoppers make sounds during the day when the Sun is hot. They rub their hind legs against ridges on their wings. This sound is quieter than a cricket chirp.

The prize for the noisiest insect goes to the cicada. On the underside of a male cicada's body are two "sound boxes" made from a substance called **chitin**. The male cicada makes an incredibly loud, piercing sound by rapidly vibrating the ribbed walls of these boxes. Often, several cicadas call from the same tree.

These insect musicians are all males, and they make their music to attract females.

Above: A male African leaf-hole cricket gnaws a hole in a leaf. It then sings through the hole.

Opposite: The wings of the male dark bush-cricket are hard and tough. When rubbed together, they make a loud chirp that can be heard over 300 feet (100 meters) away.

Above: During summer, cicada **nymphs** cast off their skins and emerge as adults.

Below: The male meadow grasshopper makes a soft, beating sound by rubbing its hind legs against its wings.

Below: The legs of the male stripe-winged grasshopper move back and forth, making a wheezy sound.

Top: A common toad carefully studies an insect before capturing it with its long tongue.

Above: A damselfly provides a delicious meal for this tree frog.

In spring, frogs and toads search for water in which to lay their eggs. In summer, frogs and toads return to land in search of food. While in the water, they do not eat. All the effort that goes into spring **spawning** makes them hungry. Fortunately, plenty of food is available in summer.

To obtain a meal, a toad performs a kind of vanishing trick. The toad sits still, with just its throat moving slightly as it breathes. The toad's huge eyes, which can see in the dark, pick up the slightest movement on the ground in front of it. A woodlouse crawls slowly toward the toad. Suddenly, the sound of a little "pop" can be heard. The woodlouse has vanished. The toad's long, sticky tongue flipped forward in the louse's direction and hauled it into the great cavern of the toad's mouth. The meal was secured with lightning speed.

Right: The tree frog does not have a long tongue, so it has to leap to catch its prey.

Left: With such an abundance of prey in summer, the green lizard eats very well.

Snakes and lizards also do most of their feeding in summer. Snakes usually kill their prey before swallowing it. Most parts of the world are home to snakes that **constrict** their prey. These types of snakes wrap their bodies around the victims and squeeze. The tight coil keeps the prey animal from breathing, and the prey suffocates. Venomous snakes inject poison into the prey with their fangs and then follow the scent trail left by the dying victims.

Below: A rat snake winds two coils around a vole to squeeze it to death. The snake then opens its **gape** and swallows the prey whole.

Gaping Mouths

Top: A house martin brings ladybugs to the nest to feed its young.

Migrant birds that winter in warm climates return to temperate regions in spring. In summer, these birds raise their chicks. Swallows and swifts feed only on flying insects, and summer is the time when these insects are most plentiful. In summer, the days are long, a further advantage for the hard-working parent birds. They have more hours of daylight in which to hunt for food for their very hungry offspring.

In fact, European swifts that live in the northerly part of their range are able to rear more chicks than swifts that live farther south. This is because summer days for the northern birds are eighteen to twenty hours long, which is longer than the days in the south.

Right: Young swallows open their yellow mouths wide. Their mother has returned home with her beak filled with insects.

Long days are not an advantage for all insect-eating birds. Swifts have cousins, called nightjars or nighthawks, that hunt insects in darkness. Nightjars' eyes are big — like owls' eyes — and their beaks gape wide to gather moths and other flying insects. Nightjars do not build nests. They lay their eggs on the ground, where both adults and babies are very well camouflaged.

The song of a nightjar is one of the most amazing sounds of summer. It is a purring type of sound that may continue for several minutes. In eastern North America, the nighttime call of the whippoorwill, a type of nightjar, is a sure sign that summer has arrived.

Above: It is summer all year for arctic terns. They breed in the north during summer there. Then, they fly south to summer in the Antarctic.

Below: A pair of gannets displays to each other.

Summer is also the time when most seabirds and waterbirds breed. Rocky cliffs, windswept beaches, and remote islands resound with birds' voices in summer. Guillemots, kittiwakes, and cormorants manage to rear their young on dangerous cliff ledges. Gannets and boobies nest in huge numbers on islands where the sound of their calls is deafening and the smell of the fish on which they feed is overpowering.

Seabirds gather together for protection. The areas they choose for breeding are safe from predators. The breeding grounds are also near the food supply, which comes from the sea.

Some nesting seabirds specialize in robbing others of their catch. A large gull will chase a fish-carrying puffin until the puffin drops its catch. The gull then swoops to catch the fish before it even hits the ground.

Left: Kittiwakes gather on rocky ledges for the summer nesting season.

To get around the problem of robbers, some of the smaller seabirds return to their nests only at night. Manx shearwaters nest in underground burrows that are difficult for them to find, even in daylight. Many of the shearwaters spend the day fishing, far out at sea. As night falls, they return to their nesting area and circle around, calling to their partners. Each bird knows the voice of its partner, so when an incoming bird hears a familiar voice replying, it knows where to land.

Left: Puffins stand guard by their nest burrows, ready to dive for cover if a predator flies past.

The Learning Curve

Top: A baby chipmunk meets a young gray squirrel. They both have a lot to learn if they are going to survive.

Above: A brown hare **leveret** is left alone by its mother at an early age. It must learn on its own what foods to eat and when to run from danger.

Right: A wolf family stays together and guards its territory. Even when the youngsters are a year old, like these, they still play with each other.

Baby mammals emerge from their nests and dens into a brand-new world in summer. They have to learn a great deal about life in a very short time or they will not survive.

Play is one of the ways in which baby **carnivores** learn hunting skills. By stalking and pouncing on their brothers and sisters, babies practice catching prey. Play also develops strong muscles and fast reactions, which youngsters need if they are to stay alive.

Young mammals do not just have to learn how to find food for themselves. They must also quickly learn to avoid danger. Many are naturally shy and will bolt for cover at the slightest sound or movement. This is an instinctive reaction. Most mammals also learn from their parents. When a

mother antelope bounds away from a predator, such as a cheetah, her baby follows and learns that cheetahs represent danger.

Baby animals also need to learn how to get along with other animals of their own species. Sometimes battles between neighboring groups of animals can be very serious. A young mammal must learn the scent of rival clans so that it can distinguish between friend and foe.

Summer is a time when plants grow rapidly and baby animals learn about survival. The weather is usually comfortable, and the natural world bustles with activity.

Activities:
Caterpillars and Kelp

Four Stages

It is difficult to imagine that a dazzling butterfly emerges from a legless and wingless pupa that looked like a curled, dead leaf.

To see how insects develop through three of their four stages, start by buying an insect cage (*above, right*) from a supplier.

You can also build a similar one from wood, glass, and gauze or mosquito netting. A cage with a 6 x 12-inch (15 x 30-centimeter) base that is 12 inches (30 cm) high will be adequate for most butterflies and moths. Ask an adult to help you make the cage. Use plywood for the base and top, and use wooden uprights to support the clear front and the gauze (mosquito-netting) sides and back. Make your cage so that the clear front slides out. Then, the gauze can be stapled to the base, top, back, and sides.

After the cage is made, the next job is to stock it. Finding caterpillars (*below*) in summer is fairly easy. Make sure you have permission to enter and collect from a natural area first. Then look for leaves that have been partly eaten because they will often lead you to caterpillars. Collect several

caterpillars in a jar (with air holes in the top). Carefully note the species of food plant on which they were feeding. Collect some of the food plant, as well. At home, hammer the cut ends of the food plant flat, and then stand the stalks in a jar of water (with the crushed ends in the water). Put the food plant in the cage. Gently place the caterpillars onto it, and keep the caterpillars supplied with food in this way.

Caterpillars are very restless when fully grown. They may pupate in the ground, among leaf litter, or suspended on plants. Put a tray of soil and some dead leaves in the cage to meet the needs of all species.

It is a wonderful thing to watch a hanging caterpillar split its skin and change into

a pupa *(opposite, bottom left)*. The most magical moment happens, however, when the adult butterfly or moth hatches.

The butterfly or moth needs to have a rough surface to climb up so that its soft, crumpled wings can expand downward *(opposite, bottom right)*.

When its wings have hardened, release your friend (and eventually, the others) and watch it fly away. The butterfly or moth will lay eggs and begin the cycle once more.

Beachcombing

The next time you walk along a beach, maybe you will see a starfish, a sea urchin, crabs' claws, fish bones, egg cases, whole fish, seeds, twigs, or driftwood. These items are often buried among seaweeds.

Seaweeds belong to a group of plants called algae. Nearly all algae grow in water. Oarweeds, or kelp, are the "trees" of the undersea world. They are anchored to the seabed by holdfasts that look like roots *(top, left)*. Storms sometimes tear entire plants loose and toss them ashore. On the beach, the leaf-like fronds of kelp rot into smelly heaps. The woody holdfasts remain, clean and sun-bleached, forming unusual and wonderful shapes *(above, right)*.

Brown seaweed that grows on rocks can be preserved by pressing the smaller fronds between layers of newspaper.

Pressed seaweed fronds make beautiful patterns when they are used as stencils with spray paints.

The delicate red seaweed that grows in shallow water can become stranded on beach pebbles *(left)*.

Make your own red seaweed display by selecting a few specimens from the water. At home, place them in a large container of water. Slide a sheet of paper under the floating fronds, and then gently lift the paper up.

Let the water slowly drain away so that each frond stays unfurled. Weigh down the edges of the paper with stones so they do not curl. Allow the paper to dry and preserve the seaweed.

Glossary

breed: to mate for the purpose of giving birth to offspring.

carbohydrate: a compound formed of carbon, hydrogen, and oxygen. Sugar is a simple carbohydrate.

carbon dioxide: a gas made of carbon and oxygen.

carnivores: animals that eat other animals.

chitin: a very tough material from which the skins of insects and many other types of animals are formed.

chlorophyll: the pigment responsible for photosynthesis and for making plants green.

condenses: changes from a vapor to a liquid (and sometimes to a solid).

constrict: to kill by squeezing.

deciduous: plants that lose their leaves during one season of the year.

dew: moisture that condenses on surfaces at night.

dew point: the conditions of temperature and humidity that are present when dew starts to form.

estivate: to spend part or all of summer in a resting state.

evaporate: to change from a liquid into a vapor.

fertilizes: causes a male cell to join with a female cell so that seeds can form or an embryo can start to grow.

gape: the line along which the jaws of an animal close.

hemisphere: one-half of Earth, divided at the Equator.

leveret: a young hare.

nymph: the young and normally wingless stage of many kinds of insects.

photosynthesis: a process in which plants use energy from the Sun to make food.

polar: refers to the areas located around the ends of Earth's axis.

pollen: male cells produced by flowers in the form of fine grains.

pupa: the stage in the life of an insect when it is changing from a larva into an adult.

saturated: carrying the maximum possible amount of water or water vapor.

solstice: the day on which the tilt of Earth's axis in relation to the Sun is the greatest.

spawning: the act of depositing eggs in order to produce young.

species: a biologically distinct type of animal or plant that can produce offspring with another member of its specific group.

temperate: refers to parts of the world between the tropics and polar regions, where the climate is without extremes.

tropics: the warm regions of the world around the Equator.

ultrasonic: sound that is too high in pitch for human hearing.

vapor: a gas formed from a liquid or solid.

Plants and Animals

The common names of plants and animals vary from language to language. Their scientific names, based on Greek or Latin words, are the same the world over. Each kind of plant or animal has two scientific names. The first name is called the genus. It starts with a capital letter. The second name is the species name. It starts with a small letter.

broad-bodied chaser dragonfly (*Libellula depressa*) — Europe 7

common tree frog (*Hyla arborea*) — southern Europe, Asia Minor to the Caspian Sea 20

common zebra (*Equus burchelli*) — southern and eastern Africa 10

crab spider (*Misumena vatia*) — Europe 14

creeping phlox (*Phlox diffusa*) — North America 6

crimson columbine (*Aquilegia formosa*) — Pacific North America 15

dark bush-cricket (*Pholidoptera griseoaptera*) on **woody nightshade** (*Solanum dulcamara*) — Europe 18-19

domestic cat (*Felis catus*) — worldwide 27

European rabbit (*Oryctolagus cuniculus*) — Europe, northern Africa; introduced to Australia, New Zealand 13

green lizard (*Lacerta viridis*) — Europe 21

mosquito (*Culex pipiens*) — worldwide 16

nightjar (*Caprimulgus europaeus*) — Europe, Asia, northern Africa 23

northern double drummer cicada (*Thopha sessiliba*) — northern Australia 19

ox-eye daisy (*Leucanthemum vulgare*) — Europe, Asia; introduced to North America 15

ponderosa pine (*Pinus ponderosa*) — western North America 11

puffin (*Fratercula arctica*) — North Atlantic 25

redwood sorrel (*Oxalis oregana*) — western North America 13

rufous hummingbird (*Selasphorus rufus*) — western North America 15

shore crab (*Carcinus maenas*) — Atlantic shores 9

Siberian chipmunk (*Eutamias sibiricus*) — Siberia, Asia; similar species North America 26

Texas rat snake (*Elaphe obsoleta*) — North America 21

topi (*Damaliscus korrigum*) — Africa 27

western anemone/pasque flower (*Anemone occidentalis*) — western North America 5

Books to Read

Bees: Busy Honeymakers. Secrets of the Animal World (series). Eulalia García (Gareth Stevens)

Butterflies. The New Creepy Crawly Collection (series). Graham Coleman (Gareth Stevens)

Flowers, Butterflies and Insects. Sally Morgan (Dover)

The Nature and Science of Sunlight. Exploring the Science of Nature (series). Jane Burton and Kim Taylor (Gareth Stevens)

Plant and Flower. David Burnie (Knopf)

Videos and Web Sites

Videos

Audubon Video: Wolves. (Vestron Video)
Butterfly and Moth. (DK Publishing)
Energy From the Sun. (Encyclopædia
    Britannica Educational Corporation)
Flowers, Plants, and Trees. (Vision Quest)
Insects. (Unapix)
Photosynthesis. (Phoenix/BFA)
The Private Life of Plants. (Turner)

Web Sites

www.geocities.com/Heartland/Hills/9659/
www.arnprior.com/kidsgarden/index.htm
www.ames.com/kids/index.html
aruba.nysaes.cornell.edu/ent/biocontrol/
    info/primer.html
www.onlinegardener.com/kids.html
horizon.nmsu.edu/garden/
db.ok.bc.ca/summer/

Some web sites stay current longer than others. For further web sites, use your search engines to locate the following topics: *bees, butterflies, photosynthesis, plants, pollination,* and *summer.*

Index